A SCATTERING OF LIGHT

INSPIRATION FOR FINDING
PEACE ON A WINDY DAY

JENNIFER WAYNE

Text & image copyright © 2012 by Jennifer Wayne

All rights reserved. No part of this book may be reproduced in any manner without written permission, except for quotations embodied in critical articles or reviews.

www.scatteringlight.net

Wayne, Jennifer
A Scattering of Light: Inspiration for Finding Peace on a Windy Day

ISBN-13: 978-1479109623
ISBN-10: 1479109622

FOR MOM AND DAD,
FOR LAUREN AND FOR DAVE,
FOR THEIR BOUNDLESS SUPPORT AND
ENCOURAGEMENT.

MAY YOU KNOW YOURSELVES BELOVED
ON THE EARTH.

AND FOR ALL THOSE WHO SEEK
PEACE ON A WINDY DAY.

TABLE OF CONTENTS

INTRODUCTION		1
1	WALLS	5
2	THE TRUTH ALWAYS SINGS TO YOU	7
3	THE SOUL'S JOURNEY	9
4	SEE THE ARROW	13
5	CHOOSE LOVE	15
6	WABI SABI	17
7	QUIET	19
8	OF EARTH & SKY	21
9	STORY TELLER	22
10	INTO THE LABYRINTH	23
11	THE ONLY WAY OUT IS THROUGH	26
12	FACE YOUR FEARS	28
13	DECIDE THAT WHAT YOU HAVE IS WHAT YOU WANT	30
14	ALLOW OTHERS TO BE THEMSELVES	32
15	WHAT WOMEN WANT	34
16	HEROES	37

17	WE LEARN BY BECOMING	40
18	CLAIM YOUR POWER	42
19	MIRRORS	44
20	CRACKED	45
21	OF DRAGONS & SIRENS	47
22	DANCE WITH DESIRE	48
23	FROM DARKNESS INTO LIGHT	49
24	EMBRACE	50
25	ECHOES	51
26	BELOVED ON THE EARTH	52
27	BEAUTY & THE BEAST	54
28	LOTUS FLOWER	57
29	GOOD LUCK, BAD LUCK	59
30	WE FIND WHAT WE SEEK	61
31	FOREVER ENTWINED	63
32	WATCH LOVE GROW	65
33	PLAYING THE GAME	67
34	ATHENA & THE OLIVE TREE	69
35	THE NATURE OF OBSTACLES	71
36	IMMORTALS	73
37	OF GODS & GODDESSES	75

38	WORTHY	77
39	OUT OF THE PAST	79
ABOUT THE AUTHOR		81

INTRODUCTION

The more time I spend on this beautiful blue-green planet, the more I understand that we are born explorers. We are fascinated by our world, by each other, by ourselves. We long to make sense of the mysteries we see without and within; we long to add our own part to the dance of life. We have so much power, to see the world as we wish to see it, to tell the stories we want to tell. To create the world we dream of creating.

But we live in a time of windstorms. Change swirls around us constantly. We long for more love, more peace and more beauty. Sometimes it feels very near to us—we feel loved and loving, whole and safe. At other times, we feel lost at sea, desperate for comfort, longing for home. We see these storms in the world around us—war, famine, poverty and economic upheaval—and in our daily lives—anxiety, illness, isolation and depression.

When our lives are going well, it is easier to be aware of the joy that surrounds us. The greater art lies in finding love and beauty even when storms are raging. As an art, it must be studied and practiced. We each possess the ability to create peace, in ourselves and in the world. It begins when we learn to find peace, not only during times of comfort, but on a windy day.

I have spent most of my life practicing peacefulness.

Those who know me might say that I was born naturally calm and balanced, that by nature I am unruffled by the world around me. I feel otherwise. There have been many times when my equilibrium was disturbed by something as minor as dry weather or as major as a lost job. But it is true that I have always been interested in cultivating peace and balance. Over the past several years, I have studied the ways of peace found by others and I have sought to learn more about myself and what keeps me grounded. When life sends storms, I seek my center. At times it seems that the stronger the storm, the easier it is to find my way back to myself, because at those moments there is no other choice. It can be the minor disturbances that prove the most challenging, and require the most practice.

When we are calm and in a place of peace, we are at our most effective. Our energy is not fragmented by fear and doubt; we are not so busy juggling a million thoughts, emotions and tasks that we miss what is right in front of us. We face adversity with quiet strength, able to know what it is we should do and how we should do it. Our peace, our balance, is a gift not only to ourselves, but to our world.

Our world is crying out for emissaries of peace. But we cannot create without what we have not cultivated within. And to do that, we must continue to practice the ways of peace, to believe in the power of harmony and balance, to value calmness and patience. We must believe that we are capable of becoming the peace we wish to see reflected in the world.

The ways of peace are many, but the simplest paths are often the surest. It is my hope that the inspiration I have found—whether from myths and legends, the philosophies of cultures and spiritual traditions around the world, or in my own musings—will be a guide for you on your own journey towards joy.

I don't have all the answers; no one does. But we all

have some. When we share those answers we have found, when we help others along their paths and accept their help in return, we stand a little taller and walk a little further. None of us journey alone. We find peace and love together, or not at all. If we all keep scattering the light we have found, we will find our way home.

> May you discover the beauty that lies in harmony.

> May you find peace on a windy day.

NOT ALL WHO WANDER ARE LOST.

J.R.R. Tolkien

JENNIFER WAYNE

1
WALLS

Time is slipping, falling like rain through the cracks in our days. We feel pain when we are afraid, when we put up walls between ourselves and the moment that is holding us. Nevertheless, we are held. We think the walls we build will make us safe, but we cannot help but build our walls out of barbed wire, rocks and broken cement. Of course they hurt us. Of course they make us less safe.

Stop protecting yourself behind walls of stone. Let the light in. Let love in. Take the walls down. Listen to the wind, read the stars and sing your stories. The world is full of sacred spaces—they are all around you. Seek them out; let them heal and refresh you. Love as a true queen loves, with beauty, grace, strength and abandon.

Everything that is not part of love is just a wall—a barrier of smoke and mirrors that obscures the truth. Know that there is nothing between your heart and soul, no barrier at all. Nothing that is not known to you, nothing that you do not possess, nothing you cannot give.

The only protection we have in this changing world is an open hand, not a closed fist. An open heart, not one buried behind walls of stone. Open, surrender, release, and know yourself immortal, divine, boundless. We are our only obstacles. Meet those parts of yourself that you would resist, meet them with love, as the friends and teachers they are, and they will dissolve like stars greeting the sunrise.

Begin where you are. Begin with what you have before

you to do and what you have within you to give.

YOUR VISION WILL BECOME CLEAR ONLY WHEN YOU
LOOK INTO YOUR HEART.
WHO LOOKS OUTSIDE, DREAMS.
WHO LOOKS INSIDE, AWAKENS.

Carl Jung

2
THE TRUTH ALWAYS SINGS TO YOU

In this moment, you are home. In this place and time, you have all you need for your journey. You are whole, and you are free.

Do you believe otherwise? Do you think your life could be, should be, different or better? Do you feel bound by obligation, constricted by expectation? Do you believe you lack time, money or love? If so, you are doing what most of us do—believing that your thoughts are true.

Our thoughts are valuable when we use them well, as the instrument they are meant to be. When we follow them blindly, without question, they lead us down a winding path of fear and confusion. Over time, as our thoughts grow louder and gain more power over us, we forget to listen to the deeper, quieter voice of our true selves. Instead, we cling to our fears and refuse to put them down. If others suggest to us that our fears are not true, we argue for them. We defend our anger and our misery.

Truth never has to be proven—it just is. The sun will rise whether or not you argue for it; the seasons will turn without you convincing anyone of that fact. Truth does not need your defense. It is your defense.

You know what is true because it sings to you. Truth makes you feel safe, expansive and powerful. It is not born of false imaginings, but of your strength and beauty.

Our thoughts, on the other hand, may be true and may not. Instead of investing them with the power of your energy and belief, trust in what is best and brightest within you. Instead of seeking counsel from your nightmares, give your power and magic to the love that binds the universe together. Trust the wisdom of your higher self and the voice that counsels love and patience. Listen to the truth that sings to you, that ignites your joy and passion, and follow where it leads.

3
THE SOUL'S JOURNEY

Psyche was a butterfly spirit; her name means "soul" or "breath." I see her standing at the top of a broad staircase, gray stone and clear windows behind her, dressed in a white gown, a red sash tied at her waist, thick curls cascading down her back. Birds and butterflies of bright blue and red surround her and flutter down the stairs below. She is the soul, awakened from a slumber of one hundred years, starting to remember that once she flew free, and that she can again. This is where the story begins, when Psyche stirs.

The legend tells us that Psyche was the most beautiful of mortals, so beautiful that the Goddess of Love and Beauty herself became jealous and commanded that the girl be taken to the top of a lonely mountain and offered up to a monster in sacrifice. And yet I wonder—is not jealousy a human emotion? Those who understand love and beauty know that both are available in abundance, that the more love and beauty we find in others, the more we ourselves possess. This could be no mystery to Aphrodite, the Goddess of Love and Beauty. And so I wonder if the command that sent Psyche up into the distant mountains alone was not, in fact, anger or punishment but merely the call to adventure, an invitation into a new life.

For once she stood upon the mountain top, far removed from the world she had known, a gentle breeze brushed past her, lifted her gown, her hair and then her very body up into the sky and away to a place beyond her most beautiful dreams. She was set gently on the ground before a golden palace, and upon exploring her new home found every nature of luxury and delight surrounding her. Lovely rooms, decadent meals and lush gardens were all her own. And at night, when the world was dark and quiet, a kind and gentle man came to her room and became her lover.

All was perfect bliss, the story tells us, until Psyche asked for and received a visit from two jealous sisters, who told her that as she had never seen her lover's face, he must be the hideous monster the Goddess had sent to bear Psyche away. But we do not need jealous sisters to raise the fear of doubt and judgment in our minds; we do that well enough for ourselves.

Whatever the cause, Psyche began to doubt. Although her eyes and heart showed her only beauty and kindness, her uncertainty grew. She wondered if the man she thought she loved and who offered every proof of his love for her might, in fact, be a hideous monster who meant her harm. The only request her lover had ever asked of her was that she never attempt to see him in the light. Nevertheless, as he lay sleeping by her side, she crept from the bed, lit an oil lamp and discovered that her sleeping lover was none other than the God of Love himself, known as Eros or Cupid. Aphrodite's son.

As she trembled in the face of love, a drop of oil spilled from the lamp and fell upon the sleeping God. He woke, saw that his love had been doubted and betrayed, and flew away into the night, leaving Psyche alone.

Without love, the beautiful palace felt empty and cold. Psyche longed for her Cupid to return, but he did not. And so Psyche began her journey into the world to find her love. She searched far and wide, with no sign of her lover. Finally, in despair, she went to a temple of Aphrodite to ask for her help, despite her belief that the Goddess despised her.

Aphrodite heard the girl's pleas and did agree to help her, but only if Psyche could complete a series of tasks. Each task was not merely difficult but impossible, seemingly designed to break Psyche's fragile spirit. They were beyond the hope of any mortal girl.

But Psyche is not, after all, just any mortal girl. She represents the soul, and when her soul is clear it reflects beauty bright enough to dazzle the God of Love himself. This beauty is not merely physical; it contains power, knowledge and a state of being that transcends the material world entirely.

The soul is never without aid if it will only ask for it. And so when Psyche cries out for help in completing one impossible task after another, the entire world conspires to aid her. Creatures great and small appear, eager to turn her tears into smiles. One by one, every task is accomplished.

Was the Goddess of Love and Beauty surprised? Did she not realize the power of her own gifts, her own domain?

Was she taken unaware? Or instead, did the Goddess know what Psyche was capable of better than the girl herself, and so devised a clever way to teach the girl her own power? When Psyche passed each of the Goddess' tests and came into full knowledge of herself, she was at last ready to stand by Cupid, the soul equal to love, the woman equal to a god.

Looking too closely at love is dangerous. It may leave us alone, afraid and confronted with impossible tasks. Yet we must question the love we find, for true love, true union and partnership, requires openness, understanding and, most of all, an understanding of ourselves, of our own gifts and power. It is only after we have dared to look reality in the face, dared to know the truth of our love and of ourselves, that we can ever hope to be truly and forever united with our desire.

Once we have seen love, our journey begins. Once we have seen love, we must follow ever after it, no matter the cost or the peril, until we are at last reunited with it forever. This is the path of the soul, different for each, but leading always to love.

And when the soul and love are finally reunited? They have a daughter, whose name is Pleasure. And the story begins again.

4
SEE THE ARROW

To find your way forward, you must know where you are, who you are and what gifts you possess. Be here now, and the future becomes not only clear but obvious. The arrow's trajectory is never a mystery to one who truly sees the arrow.

We possess many different gifts. The one we all share is truth. We are truth. That is our gift, not to receive, but to give. To share. But we cannot give from a place of weakness. We can only give from our truest, most authentic selves. We have nothing else to give, but our authentic selves. Being ourselves, loving ourselves, loving others, loving each moment—that is how we heal ourselves, one another and the world.

Are you afraid? To be afraid is human. You cannot stifle fear, cannot sneak past it. What you can do is accept it, learn what you can from it and then choose the path of love instead. Even in the face of fear, the face of defeat, failure and destruction, you must always choose love. That is the only lesson worth learning, the only test before you. That is what all true stories teach—that it is possible to choose love. That love is the only answer, and the only hope.

THIS PLACE WHERE YOU ARE RIGHT NOW,
GOD CIRCLED ON A MAP FOR YOU.

Hafiz

A SCATTERING OF LIGHT

5
CHOOSE LOVE

Our lives are given shape and meaning by those things on which we choose to put our attention. We can seek the good, the beautiful, the things that bring us comfort and joy, or we can focus on what causes us pain, what frightens us, what makes us angry.

We think we should seek out pain, to defend ourselves against it. All that does is allow the pain to expand, to consume us, to drive our actions and encourage us to close our hearts. It makes us worry; it makes us forget all that we love. We create the very things we fear. We all have a choice between love and fear; the trick is to remember to make a choice, rather than be blown about by a changing world.

There is a Native American legend about a wise elder who described the struggle this way: "Within me, there are two dogs. One is good; the other is mean and evil. The evil dog is constantly attacking the good dog."

"Which dog," asked a child, "will win?"

After a moment's reflection, the elder replied: "The one I feed the most."

So feed those parts of you that are patient, forgiving and kind. Search for joy. Be grateful for the sun on your skin, the rain on the earth and the wind in the trees. Let yourself love. Let yourself sing. Remember how to dance. Then watch your soul expand, and the world with it.

6
WABI SABI

Nothing is perfect. Nothing is finished. Nothing is permanent. But everything is part of love.

The Japanese art and philosophy of Wabi Sabi teaches us to embrace and celebrate the imperfect, the unfinished and the impermanent. To notice that it is the crack in the vase that gives it character and beauty; that lets in the light. We suffer when we deny this, when we try to make things fixed, permanent and perfect. Those of us who reach for perfection, who want to capture time and hold it motionless, miss the glory of change, the gift of evolution. The magic that lies in the mystery of transformation.

There is no reason to fear change, no reason to force motionlessness on a dancing world. If you would be happy, learn to appreciate what is unique, what is changing, what is still left undone. Instead of trying to capture the world, learn to dance with it.

It is the hidden beauty that connects us most powerfully to what is true and divine. For who can ever know what is perfect and what is a flaw? A closer look often reveals that a flaw is actually an object's—a person's—greatest strength and beauty. What we call a flaw is merely an invitation to look deeper.

Can you be sure that what you see, hear and feel is a flaw, and not the very essence of beauty?

A SCATTERING OF LIGHT

7
QUIET

    Wisdom creeps near when it finds one who is sitting, listening, opening. It is like a small creature of the forest, frightened away by loud noises, by loud thoughts; drawn only to the beauty that dares to visit alone. It trusts only those who are still, patient and open; those who will greet vulnerability with love.

    Our dreams are a field of butterflies: numerous, fragile, impossible to contain. But some are worth catching. The ones nearest our own souls will slow down their flight, wait for us to catch up and wrap a net of pen and paper around them. They will not fly away, not if we sing them our stories. Not if we promise to listen well.

What song do they sing?

Live now. Be here now. Be radiant now.

Can you see that this is Heaven?

All of our transformations begin within. The external world follows the soul, not the other way around. Some say our world is an illusion; I believe it is a mirror, a reflection offering us the chance to learn, to grow and to explore. As our souls grow and expand, our worlds grow with them, for we are one.

Be open to change. Say yes, and give thanks. Then keep listening to the quiet voice of wisdom that lives within your heart.

A BIRD DOESN'T SING BECAUSE IT HAS AN ANSWER.
IT SINGS BECAUSE IT HAS A SONG.

Dr. Maya Angelou

8
OF EARTH & SKY

A tree needs both roots and branches. It cannot choose one over the other or it will die. It must be forever of both earth and sky. That is balance, harmony and union. We must live the same way, never denying any part of ourselves. Reach and rest. Sleep and wake. Fall and rise. Sink into the earth and listen to the wind. Be nourished and nourish others.

Do not hold back. Do not save your brilliance, your wisdom or your joy. Live now. Be who you are now. Do not wait. Do not hesitate. Stop holding so tightly to the very things you don't want: doubt of yourself and your path, fear of the future. Let go, and let the world in. You are loved, just as you are.

The future tends to itself. Never before has it allowed you to usurp that role; it will not now. Remember: what you desire also desires you.

9
STORY TELLER

We are all stories. We move through our lives like storybook heroes and heroines, facing villains, seeking the aid of wise counselors, searching for treasure. We pin together the moments of our lives by telling ourselves stories, by imagining that the thread of the tale is consistent and meaningful. It is a safety device, a way to feel some measure of control over our days.

Our stories are not truth, although in our fascination we often think they are. What is true is what lies beyond the stories, beyond the dramas, behind our thoughts: the mystery. The eternal. The real. Some call it mindlessness, but only because we lack the words to describe the indescribable. And so we continue to tell our stories, to live our lives as stories. Until the day when we see past it all. Until we are able to connect with our true and eternal selves, and know ourselves home at last.

We are the mystery we seek.

10
INTO THE LABYRINTH

Ariadne was a princess of Crete, daughter of Minos, the king that created the labyrinth that housed the Minotaur. The Minotaur, half-man and half-bull, was the son of a pure white bull and the queen, Ariadne's mother. He was a monstrous creature who devoured innocent men and women, and so was imprisoned within a dark and twisting labyrinth far beneath the palace.

The hero Theseus arrived from Athens intent on destroying the monster. For love of him, the princess Ariadne betrayed her father and family and promised the hero her help. She gave Theseus a ball of red thread, and told him that if he would unwind it as he made his way through the labyrinth, he would then be able to follow the thread out again.

Did Theseus need the red thread? Or was Ariadne's gift one of hope and comfort? A labyrinth, unlike a maze, is not always a place of dead-ends and twisting turns. A labyrinth may be a direct, although curving, journey to the center of the self, a winding path that is nevertheless sure in its destination and in the return. It is, in fact, a mirror of our own lives. We can see ourselves as lost in a frightening maze, unsure of the terrors around the next corner. Or we can see ourselves in a true labyrinth, in which we cannot see what lies ahead but know we will ultimately be led to the center of our souls, and back again. The fact that we cannot see what is coming next is the gift of time.

We fear that, buried deep within our souls, far below the realm of our daily lives, there lives within us a beast, an unknown aspect of ourselves that cannot be controlled. But into the labyrinth we must go, as Theseus did, to face the part of ourselves that we would hide.

Whatever the Minotaur represents, and whether his home was a maze or a labyrinth, Theseus took Ariadne's thread with him and was able to slay the beast. On finding his way safely out, from darkness into the light, he stole away with Ariadne, sailing back towards Athens with the promise that he would make her his wife.

Then he left her, alone and sleeping, on the shore of a small island. Some versions of the tale say he was swept away in a storm, in grief over her loss; others that he had no care for her and abandoned her at the first opportunity. And yet other versions claim that he was forced to leave by the God of Wine, Dionysus, who loved her and desired her for himself.

When Ariadne awoke, alone on the sandy beach, she thought herself abandoned and betrayed, whatever the reality might have been. She had left her family, her home and her life, to sail away with a man who did not or could not love her as she loved him. She did not realize that, whatever Theseus' intent, a better future awaited her. One in which she was the chosen, the beloved, of a god, brought into the heavens and made a goddess in her own right. Her wedding crown, the

Corona, was placed in the night sky as a constellation, as a tribute to the endless love between Dionysus and Ariadne.

Like Psyche, Ariadne could not have known what future awaited her; none of us can. But it is usually better than we could ever hope or imagine.

ONE THING THAT COMES OUT IN MYTHS IS THAT AT THE BOTTOM OF THE ABYSS COMES THE VOICE OF SALVATION.
THE BLACK MOMENT IS THE MOMENT WHEN THE REAL MESSAGE OF TRANSFORMATION IS GOING TO COME.
AT THE DARKEST MOMENT COMES THE LIGHT.

Joseph Campbell

11
THE ONLY WAY OUT IS THROUGH

    To hold to our center through all the changes brought by tide or time. To feel at ease in all places, with all people, with all parts of ourselves. At what price comes such freedom?

    There are no maps, and no reason to create one. Create

instead a song to dance to, one that will serve as a reminder of light when the way seems darkest. Then weave the wind into starlight.

Every leaf and branch twirls with love for us. Or is it our love for them, stirring the wind itself to life? Which came first, and does it matter? Is there any difference at all? Love leads itself home, by any path presented to it.

We search for places the wind cannot go, not realizing that such places cannot exist, and that if they did they would be more hollow than graveyards.

The only way out is through.

What adventure will you follow today? How will you journey? Will you fall into yourself and let joy have you, or will you strive and strain and try? Don't. Oh, please, don't. If you feel that you are alone in a dark room, it is only because you have closed your eyes. Open them.

In the center of our lives there is a star, the light of love itself, our only true guide and always a gentle, patient one. It does not rule or command us, but it goes where the way is darkest, the pain is deepest, to heal through the power of gentleness, teaching us to transform our lives and worlds with an open heart.

12
FACE YOUR FEARS

Let yourself feel what haunts you. Face the monster in the labyrinth.

There is no need to hide from your suffering, no reason to shut out pain. Most fears, most worries, exist only in our minds, a realm over which we possess absolute power, if only we dare to claim it. But you cannot conquer what you do not allow yourself to see.

How can we overcome our fears when we hide from

them? How can we find the strength we need to dare, to explore, to try or to love when all of our energy is busy building walls between us and those parts of ourselves we would deny? Even your weaknesses will become strengths when you claim them as your own. They will either teach you where you need to journey next, or help you heal the fragmented parts of your soul.

Face enough of the monsters you dread, and you will learn that they are all teachers and guides. They teach you about your strength, your fortitude and your ability to choose tolerance and compassion. They show you what you must overcome to be free. In the end, they teach you that they do not exist at all, and that there is nothing you need to fear.

13
DECIDE THAT WHAT YOU HAVE IS WHAT YOU WANT

Peace and happiness can only be found where you are. They do not exist in the future or the past, because right here and now, neither of those places exist. What you have to work with, what you have to create with, is this. Wherever you are. Whatever time it is. Whatever mood you are in and however you are feeling. This is it. And one simple way to make whatever it is even better is to decide that what you have is what you want.

Not someday. Not if only. As it is. Start by finding something good, even something small. If you're single, you have time and space for yourself. If you're stuck in a dead-end job, you have an income. If you don't feel well, you have a body that's telling you to rest and nurture yourself. If you have no idea where to go or what to do, then anything is possible and the adventure is about to begin. Start small, and grow from there. Start by pretending, if you need to.

You may find, to your surprise, that what you have actually *is* what you want. When you stop judging yourself, stop looking to some imagined ideal of how life "should" look or how things "should" be, you may find that what you have is exactly the right life for the unique person you are. Try to see things that way; question the truth of what you think you don't want. Make the decision that will lead you back to peace.

14
ALLOW OTHERS TO BE THEMSELVES

You are free to live as you choose to live, to be as you want to be. Believe that, and believe that others have the equal right to navigate their own lives. This is the secret to finding peace in relationships.

Accepting others as they are, allowing them to be their own unique and changing selves, is the greatest gift one can give another. Give others permission to be themselves and you give yourself the same gift. We are all sovereign of our lives. It is only when we doubt that, when we think that others can control us or that we should control them, that we make relationships contentious and complicated, based upon fear rather than love.

We grow and change all the time, and so it is no

wonder that many relationships that began in love end in sadness and anger. What began as interest in others, in learning about their uniqueness, their hopes and dreams, their true selves, becomes something else to control. We judge those we claim to love most. Love is destroyed.

Instead of destroying that which you treasure, learn to treat your lover as a friend, and the world entire as your beloved. When you realize that all the love in the world is already yours, there is nothing you need cling to. You are not dependent on anyone for your happiness. You can join with others as lovers, playmates and friends, and as you and they grow and change you have nothing to fear, because you have no expectations or demands.

If you would heal your relationships, if you would know true love with the ones dearest to you, then love them as they are. Love them as they change. Give them the freedom to journey as their souls dictate. And know that no matter how tightly you are bound to another, you always have the same freedom.

YOUR TASK IS NOT TO SEEK FOR LOVE, BUT MERELY TO SEEK AND FIND ALL THE BARRIERS WITHIN YOURSELF THAT YOU HAVE BUILT AGAINST IT.

Rumi

15
WHAT WOMEN WANT

There is a story that answers the oldest of questions: what do women want?

A young and handsome knight of Camelot, named Gawain, set out to find the answer to save King Arthur from losing his throne. It sounds perilous—an entire kingdom dependent on determining what women want. But for a true knight, all things are possible. Answers always present themselves to those who honestly seek them.

For Sir Gawain, the answer presented itself in the guise of an old woman. She appeared in the forest, withered by age and sickness, and asked him for food. Being a kind as well as noble knight, Gawain made a place for her by the warm fire and gave her his food and drink. In gratitude, she told Gawain that she knew of his quest and would give him the answer he sought, if he would take her back to Camelot and make her his wife.

This was a harsh fate for a strong, handsome young man, the prize of the court and the favorite of all the beautiful young ladies. But Arthur's kingdom was at stake, and so Gawain could do nothing but agree.

Upon his promise to marry her, she told him the secret of what all women want—to have their own way. But the story does not end there.

Gawain and his promised bride returned to Camelot, and the entire court grieved at seeing the young man bound to a haggard old woman, wise though she might be. But the wedding was duly planned and celebrated in lavish style, and that night Gawain joined his new bride in their wedding chamber.

When the court had retired and the couple was alone, a miraculous thing occurred—glowing light surrounded the wise woman, and then her form shifted and changed into that of a stunning young beauty with flowing blonde hair and cornflower blue eyes.

"I was cursed by an evil magician," the lady said, "and forced to walk the world as an old woman before my time, until and unless a knight of Arthur's court would make me his wife. But I am afraid the curse is not completely broken, and a choice is before you, my husband. You must choose—would you have me beautiful by day, when all the court could see me, or at night, when we are alone together in our bedchamber? What, my husband, would you desire?"

"I cannot decide," Gawain declared, after a moment's thought. "You must choose which is more pleasing to you."

"And now," cried his lady, "the curse is well and truly broken, and I am free to appear as my true self at all hours of the day and night, for you have given me what all women wish for—the ability to have my own way."

It is not only women, of course, who long to have their own way. For what does it mean, to have one's own way, but to be one's true and authentic self, at all times and in all places? This is the gift of love that breaks all curses, and sets us free.

16
HEROES

Heroes travel on the wind, as we all must. So what is it that makes them heroes? Simply this: they choose love, even when fear and pain surround them. They know who they are and can sense their mission, their purpose, even when all seems dark and cold. They may stumble and lose their way, they may forget and they may doubt. Yet when the road is darkest, when all seems lost, they find their way. They stand up, walk on and continue. When the world becomes dark and quiet, then they can listen, then they can see. They rise again, and again, and continue on.

We are all heirs of a mythical past, and guardians of forgotten truth. The world calls to each of us, over and over again. Some are waiting for the call, listening intently for it. Others are awakened suddenly by it. Still others resist, ignore or deny the call. The tapestry of the future is woven all the same.

We are the chosen ones. We would not have been born if we did not have unique, irreplaceable, powerful purposes for being here. The universe does not waste space, does not make mistakes. Do not fear over-reaching; you cannot. Do not ask if you are worthy of the path you see before you; you could not see it if it were not meant for you. You are divine, an immortal at play in a human world. Ride the wave that moves between your humanity and your divinity, play the part you long to play. Embrace all the facets of your starlit soul.

You will always be given the tools you need, once you

begin the quest. Such is the way of the world, always and without fail. Even your failures will provide the key to your freedom. Such is the way of love.

IT IS NOT BECAUSE THINGS ARE DIFFICULT THAT WE DO NOT DARE;
IT IS BECAUSE WE DO NOT DARE THAT THEY ARE DIFFICULT.

Seneca

WE HAVE NOT EVEN TO RISK THE ADVENTURE ALONE, FOR THE HEROES OF ALL TIME HAVE GONE BEFORE US—THE LABYRINTH IS THOROUGHLY KNOWN.

WE HAVE ONLY TO FOLLOW THE THREAD OF THE HERO PATH, AND WHERE WE HAD THOUGHT TO FIND AN ABOMINATION, WE SHALL FIND A GOD; WHERE WE HAD THOUGHT TO SLAY ANOTHER, WE SHALL SLAY OURSELVES; WHERE WE HAD THOUGHT TO TRAVEL OUTWARD, WE SHALL COME TO THE CENTER OF OUR OWN EXISTENCE.

AND WHERE WE HAD THOUGHT TO BE ALONE, WE SHALL BE WITH ALL THE WORLD.

Joseph Campbell

17
WE LEARN BY BECOMING

YOU HAVE SUFFERED ONLY FOR THIS:
THAT YOU MAY BLESS OTHERS WHO SUFFER STILL.

Haven Trevino

We learn by becoming. There is no other way. We cannot think our way through the world; we cannot heal others or ourselves by pretending to live. We are here to feel, to grow and to change. To experience all facets of life, of being human.

Sometime our changes are abrupt and earth-shattering; at other times they happen so slowly we don't notice until later that we have been reborn into a new life, a new world. Either way, one day we will look back and know that our journeys have been perfect all along, that every step taken was blessed. All we lacked was eyes with which to see it.

Do not worry because you feel alone. Do not worry because you are afraid. Even heroes doubt their paths, doubt their choices, doubt their callings. That is natural. That is human. It does not mean you have failed. It only means you have forgotten.

And when we forget, when we think that our fears are real and eternal, when we feel sorrow and pain, then we learn compassion for others. And it is only through our compassion for others that we can find peace.

Allow yourself to feel, allow yourself to heal, and then bless those who suffer still.

18
CLAIM YOUR POWER

The ancient myths and legends are full of tales of rightful kings and queens who lost their thrones and struggled to reclaim them. It was believed, in ancient times, that the right to rule was given by God and any pretender to the throne could never be more than that—a pretender. The true king or queen always retained the right to rule and, in the end, was always restored to his or her throne.

This is true for all of us—no one but ourselves has the right to rule our lives. No one else can or should. No matter what situation we find ourselves in, no matter how dark or terrible, no one can take from us the decision of how to react, of how to face the challenges before us. We all have that right and freedom, and it cannot be taken away.

Not many of us realize our power. We think usurpers besiege us at every turn. We think that others are trying to control us—our families, friends, partners—even strangers we meet on the street. We think we have no control over our lives, and so we doubt our power and suspect others of stealing it from us. We keep our guard up. We fear others who require our time and attention; we fear manipulation.

And perhaps sometimes we are right—some people may attempt to take our power from us, to prove their own strength by claiming what is not theirs. But no matter how much they try, no one can take your power from you. Not ever. Return to the truth. No one rules your life but you. You are the one and only trueborn king or queen of your personal kingdom. Even if you have forgotten your power for years, it is still yours, and you can always reclaim it.

The choice is yours. Anne Frank chose to find beauty out of one small window that let in daylight. Victor Frankel chose to bring compassion and sympathy into his experience of the Holocaust. We may not be able to control life, but we are always able to control what part we play in it.

It follows naturally that every other person on this planet is also sovereign of his or her own life. You cannot usurp the power others have over their lives any more than they can usurp yours. So let them rule their own lives. Even when it is your child, your spouse, your best friend—trust that they are the one true sovereign of their world, just as you are the one true sovereign of yours. You may think you know better than they do, but you couldn't possibly. It is not your domain.

Awareness of your own power, and of the equal power of others, is what brings peace to relationships. We no longer try to control others or fear that they will control us. We meet as equals, the rulers of two kingdoms coming together, perhaps sharing stories, lending advice or aid, but never trying to take what cannot be taken, or defend what cannot be lost.

19
MIRRORS

Stories are our mirrors, truer mirrors than those made of glass. They show us who we are, and who we hope to be. They help us to see, to understand, to make sense of our lives and our journeys. They create connections between us and our worlds.

True stories are the oldest form of alchemy. When a story weaves and wraps itself around your soul you are forever altered. The world will never look the same again, will never be the same again. The stories that haunt you are reflections of yourself.

So how do you sing the song of your life? Do you choose to tell your story as the ancient bards did, crafting stories that heal, refresh, teach and counsel? Are you the hero or the victim, the child or the king?

We all create mirrors. Choose yours wisely, and then do not be afraid to look deeply into the glass.

A SCATTERING OF LIGHT

20
CRACKED

There was once a crack in the mirror of a powerful and beautiful queen. When she looked into the glass, seeking confirmation of her beauty, she saw instead the image of another: Snow White. Because of the crack in the mirror—a crack in her own soul—she did not understand what she saw. She did not realize that what we see in others is a reflection of ourselves.

We doubt our power when we forget to use it. We doubt our beauty when we look for it outside of ourselves. And so the queen believed that her youth and beauty were gone

45

to another, and determined to kill the young Snow White. But Snow White was the image the queen saw when she looked into the glass—how could she kill Snow White without killing a part of herself?

As for Snow White, the queen's pursuit sent her on a journey of discovery. She began as a victim, alone and hunted through a dark forest, and emerged a queen in her own right, sure of her own strength and power. Two faces in the glass; two journeys of discovery. Both are two sides of the same coin. We all have power and beauty within us. When we see the gifts of others as a part of our own light, our power and beauty grow. When we see others as separate, as a threat, an enemy to be destroyed, we can only destroy ourselves.

We are surrounded by mirrors, constantly reminded of who we are and what we have within us. The beauty you see in others is a reflection of the beauty that is within you. The power you see in others is a reflection of the power that lies within you. The whole world is your mirror. Instead of asking who is the fairest of them all, ask instead to understand that the fairest is the one who sees beauty in others as well as in him or herself.

21
OF DRAGONS & SIRENS

Peace is not freedom from pain, but transcendence.

Pain can be an invitation, a call to adventure, an opportunity to forgive and to heal. No one lives free from pain; no one can help but cause pain. We all must, at times, play the muse to another's story, whether we intend to or not. Think of them—the evil stepmothers, the dragons and the sirens. They are the ones who send the call, who propel the heroes and heroines into the realm of adventure and possibility. They are the ones who open the door to the bright, messy world we call life. They are the fire of change. Why fear playing the part of fire?

Play your part as openly and truthfully as you know how, choose love over fear and be quick to forgive.

22
DANCE WITH DESIRE

What is it that you desire? What do you long for? Do you enjoy your desires, secure in the knowledge that all you could ever want or need will be yours? Or do you struggle against them, deny them, find in your longings an excuse to suffer and focus on what you lack?

Understand the true nature of your desires: they show you who you are, and who you want to be. There is no reason for jealousy or suffering. Look around you—so often what we want we have already, for love, abundance and beauty come in endless forms. If not, know that your desires are your guide, leading you toward the future. Perhaps not the future you expect, perhaps not the exact replica of your visions, but nevertheless a glimpse into what is forming around you.

What we desire most is to feel. The desired object, experience or person is not so deeply longed for as the feeling of love, safety, peace, adventure or passion. Feelings are our truest, deepest desires. Locate the truth of your dream, and the ways to fulfill it will be limitless. Problems will become possibilities, a chance to use your creativity and vision.

Open your heart to your desires. Let them teach you who you are and who you may be. Know that they are yours, waiting for you to claim them.

23
FROM DARKNESS INTO LIGHT

There is nothing you cannot love. There is nothing that does not already love you.

Would you transform darkness into light? Then find the beauty that already exists around and within you. Let your inner wisdom guide you; tap into your spirit, your love and your strength. That is your true compass, not the shadows you see in the night.

Dare to feel what hurts and what heals. Don't cling to life or push it away. Love what is in you to love. Do what is before you to do. Be who it is in you to be.

24
EMBRACE

Once you have truly seen something—seen into its heart and understood it—you can never fail to see it again. It is always there, always whispering, always waiting. It is the awakened Beloved.

Find the quiet beauty, the hidden perfection. Let yourself be guided by truth. How do you know when you are hearing the voice of truth? It does not taste of fear. It does not blame, reject or accuse. It forgives. It is kind. It is the best in you, the best in others. And it is always there, waiting for you to choose love over fear, hoping that you will listen.

So put all of your eggs in one basket. Stop hedging your bets. Give your all to love, light and hope. And remember: your life is not yours to fix. It is yours to embrace.

ACT AS IF YOU TRUST YOUR GOD.

Anonymous

25
ECHOES

Echoes of the future, echoes of the past, meet here, in the present. What better home could you have? What will you create next, along with the Universe? What game will you play? How will you love? How will you dance? What will you grow into, and what stories will you tell about it?

Wake up, and all things are possible. Love is endless. We are divine and free. In this moment, hold eternity and know its name: Love.

It is not a mystic's dream or a poet's wit to say that all can be found in this moment. What is this moment but the meeting ground of past and present? They greet one another like old friends, easy in each other's company. In this moment lie all the secrets of the world—of all worlds. But know this: you are not the unraveller of secrets. You are the secret. That is why there can never be an end to mystery.

You know in your heart that, as with all good secrets, the joy lies in the search, the adventure, the discovery. What lies at the end of your searching is, whatever else it might be, an ending. And for heroes, storytellers and dreamers, those are always better left unhurried.

26
BELOVED ON THE EARTH

AND DID YOU GET WHAT YOU WANTED FROM THIS
LIFE, EVEN SO?
I DID.
AND WHAT DID YOU WANT?
TO CALL MYSELF BELOVED, TO FEEL MYSELF BELOVED
ON THE EARTH.

Raymond Carver

The whole world conspires to teach you only this: you are Spirit, beloved of Spirit. All your journeys lead to truth; all your wanderings bring you home. All we seek is to come closer to that realization, to know ourselves and the Beloved more deeply, more fully.

You need not reach for love—you are the body and soul of love itself. Would you look for music? Would you listen for sunlight?

Follow love. Do neither too much nor too little. There is only one thing we must practice: how to love more deeply, more openly, more completely. More fearlessly. Those who look with the eyes of love see more deeply and more truly.

The world loves you as much as you love it; perhaps even more so. So let yourself love. Let the world in, and yourself out.

27
BEAUTY & THE BEAST

    Once upon a time, a woman so kind, so pure, so lovely that her very name was Beauty was taken prisoner by a hideous Beast. Through time, Beauty grew to love the Beast, and her love transformed him into a prince.

    Like all true stories, the tale of Beauty and the Beast may be understood various ways. The first, the most common reading, is that the love of a good woman can turn even a beast into a prince. This is the secret gift of love—that its presence awakens all of us, brings us from darkness into light. When we know we are loved, we know we are free to be our true selves, our most authentic, most wise, most lovable selves. When we feel the touch of love, we are transformed.

Another reading of the story is that the Beast represents a part of Beauty herself, the unknown and denied animal nature within, the subconscious, the primal. To be fully whole and free, Beauty must learn to accept this part of herself, her darkness as well as her light, as we all must. Only by accepting and loving the darker parts of herself can Beauty come into her true power and grace.

But I see an even greater lesson hidden within this tale. As I see it, the Beast represents the whole world, the whole universe.

At the beginning of the tale, Beauty finds herself in a strange world governed, she thinks, by a monster. Everyone else—her family, the townspeople—tells her that the Beast is a monster and that she is not safe with him. When she looks at him, she sees what she expects to see, what everyone has told her to see—a Beast. And yet, the Beast is kind to her. Gentle. He gives her everything she could ever wish for, every comfort, every pleasure. Even, when she asks for it, her freedom. The reality of the Beast is far from Beauty's expectation, far from the claims of the outside world.

When Beauty finally sees with her own eyes and heart the reality of the Beast's love, she sees the truth that was there all along—that the Beast is a handsome prince, and that she is his beloved.

Life is much like this. We come into the world terrified, and we learn from our family and friends that the world is a cruel place full of suffering. We are afraid, we think ourselves alone. And yet, if we only open our eyes and our hearts, what do we see? We see trees, oceans and flowers—beauty spread across the earth. We feel the warmth of the sun and feel the arms of our loved ones. We hear birds sing and children laugh. If we look deeper, trust in love rather than in fear, we see there is no end to the beauty and love that surround us. We see that even freedom is ours, if we choose it, for the ultimate freedom, the freedom to be our true and authentic selves, has never been denied us. We see the beauty of the world, and we know ourselves beloved, just as Beauty did.

This is the secret: We are Beauty. We are Beloved. But we can only see what we are. We must find the beauty within before we can find it without.

THOUGH WE TRAVEL THE WORLD OVER TO FIND THE BEAUTIFUL,
WE MUST CARRY IT WITHIN US,
OR WE FIND IT NOT.

Robert Waldo Emerson

28
LOTUS FLOWER

Pure beauty, floating serenely on water sparkling with light, does not begin its journey warm, cradled, safe. No, its roots lie far below the surface, in the dark, cold mud of the earth. Its seed lies dormant, often for many years. One day it pushes up, through the mud, through the dark, and reaches the light above. Only then does it bloom, full of beauty, a symbol of peace and enlightenment.

A lotus flower is not beautiful in spite of the mud, but because of it. It is the earth that gives it the strength to journey towards the light. We are the same—it is our past, our struggles and our darker experiences that teach us our abilities. That send us on our journeys toward love. We learn to reach for the light, to express our beauty, only after we have traveled through times of darkness and uncertainty.

We do not always see our paths. We do not see the evolving, unfinished design. Yet the Designer does not fail us. Trust. Accept. Practice faith. Or don't, and that will be part of the journey, too.

There will come a time, a time beyond time, when we will be one with ceaseless, passionate joy. Until then, embrace the uncertainty. Embrace the many-faceted experiences of your life, for none will ever come quite the same way again. Love it all, even when love seems distant and cold. It never is.

29
GOOD LUCK, BAD LUCK

There is a Chinese proverb about a farmer whose horse escaped into the hills. His neighbors sympathized with the farmer over his bad luck, but the farmer said: "Bad luck? Good luck? Who knows?" A week later, the horse returned, and brought with him a herd of wild horses. The neighbors now said: "What good luck!" But the farmer replied: "Good luck? Bad luck? Who knows?"

The next week, the farmer's son was attempting to tame one of the wild horses, fell off the horse, and broke his leg. "What bad luck!" said the neighbors. But a week later, an army marched into the village and conscripted every able-bodied young man they found into service. The farmer's son was spared. "What good luck!"

We can never judge good luck from bad until the tale is

complete. And what tale is ever finished?

THEY MUST OFTEN CHANGE, WHO WOULD BE
CONSTANT IN HAPPINESS OR WISDOM.

Confucius

30
WE FIND WHAT WE SEEK

We see a world that conforms to our expectations, our hopes and our fears. When our minds and hearts are open, anything is possible. When we are determined to see what we expect to see, the world obliges us by fulfilling our demands. Our fears are realized. Determined to prove ourselves right, we find the evidence that supports our expectations.

Do we need to be right? There is so much to explore, so much to discover. There is so much we do not know. Nothing is finished or perfect, including our understanding of the universe, of where we are from, of where we are going. And that imperfect understanding means there is always more to discover, more to learn, more to be.

Endless joy.

IF WE COULD SEE THE MIRACLE OF A SINGLE FLOWER CLEARLY, OUR WHOLE LIFE WOULD CHANGE.

Buddha

A SCATTERING OF LIGHT

31
FOREVER ENTWINED

Stop. Here and now. Let yourself open, let yourself feel. This moment will never come again. Embrace it. Embrace the wabi sabi nature of the world and of your life. This is meditation.

Meditation is not another project for your to-do list. It is not something else you need to do or obtain to prove yourself spiritual. Many people meditate to be calmer, more patient, more enlightened—and this may be the result—but the real reason to meditate is simply to allow what is to be. To allow yourself to be. To rest in the now. Not so that you can check "enlightenment" off your list. Not so that you can

63

achieve some standard of perfection you have set for yourself. But rather, so that you can learn to embrace imperfection.

Wabi Sabi teaches us that everything is imperfect, impermanent and unfinished. We spend most of our time ignoring or denying that fact. We either cling to what is before us—our relationships, our possessions, those things we think we want—or we push it all away, hold it at arm's length, because we know it cannot last. Meditation is an opportunity to practice a different way, a way that neither clings to what is nor denies it.

When we meditate (which is to say, when we are firmly rooted in the present moment), we allow ourselves to experience what is before us. We really feel the wind in our hair, we taste the blackberry melting on our tongues, we allow the colors of the grass and flowers to flood our eyes. No moment will ever come again in quite the same way, but when you allow a moment to fill your senses, when you experience it fully, it becomes a part of you. You may not remember it later, but you do not need to. It is you, and you are it, forever.

This is why it is not important how you meditate. How long, where, with what tools—these are all just guides to lead you into the here and now. What matters is that you open, and open again, and again.

We forget, in the rush of our lives, to be present. We fall back into our old habits of clinging and pushing, clinging and pushing. With meditation, we practice being, accepting, allowing. We train ourselves to see the world differently, to experience our lives differently. We learn to delight in the changes, rather than fear them. We learn to love what is, even as it moves and transforms. And finally, we allow ourselves to merge with time and space, forever entwined, a dance without beginning or end.

32
WATCH LOVE GROW

How we do anything is how we do everything.

Do everything with love.

It is always a choice, and one that must be made again and again. Others may not notice. If they do, they may think that the choice to love, to be patient, to forgive, was easy—easier than battling, easier than fighting. It is true that it gets easier. But choosing to love is the path of heroes, not the path of least resistance.

Who we are is expressed in every single thing we do, in each moment of the night and day. So often we forget who we are and instead react to what is around us—we meet impatience with impatience, anger with anger, rather than letting our true natures shine through.

Think of a sunflower—no matter what is going on around it, a sunflower takes in sunlight and water and turns it into beauty. It does not bloom for some and not for others. It shares what it is with everyone. Be like a flower, spreading love and light—even to those who might not deserve it. You will feel better, they will feel better, and moment by moment the world will grow in beauty and light.

Keep turning towards the light, the way a flower follows the sun. See the clouds as an opportunity to shine, rather than an excuse to despair. Act always from your true nature, your beauty, your kindness and your truth, and watch

JENNIFER WAYNE

love grow around you.

33
PLAYING THE GAME

**WE DON'T STOP PLAYING BECAUSE WE GROW OLD;
WE GROW OLD BECAUSE WE STOP PLAYING.**

George Bernard Shaw

The older we get, the more consumed we are by work. We want to do more, have more and accomplish more. We think that all these things will make us happy. Someday. We think that by doing things that don't make us happy, by suffering for our duties and obligations, we will earn our happiness. But, intuitively, we know better. We know that happiness follows joy, not suffering.

Why this preoccupation with how diligent we are, how focused, how much we suffer for duty? Why not, instead, pride yourself on how much fun you are having? Or, better still, on how much fun you can make your work?

When I worked in the corporate world, the days that flowed the best were the ones in which I embraced my job and treated it like a game, rather than resenting and struggling against it. Dressed in my suit, briefcase in one hand and a coffee in the other, on my way to another oh-so-important meeting... I was playing at being a lawyer. Some might say that this isn't a serious way to approach a career, yet those were the days that I was at my brightest, quickest, most capable and hard-working. I was not succumbing to stress and fear. I embraced the game, and I played it well. The most successful lawyers I know are the ones who enjoy practicing law, who see the fun in it. Is that so surprising? Those who enjoy what they do always do it best.

Is it so different from what we learned as children? We dressed up and pretended to be teachers, soldiers and hairdressers. Even the most ordinary and mundane professions seemed glamorous and exciting. We couldn't wait for the day when it was real. Yet when that day came, we started to take our lives seriously, and lost the fun of the game.

What we really desire is to keep playing. To make the difficult, challenging and boring moments of our lives interesting, exhilarating, an adventure. And why not? Why not change your point of view, and embrace the game rather than the fear? Whatever you do with your day—work in an office, care for children, serve drinks, cook dinner—make it a game. Use your creativity, your sense of wonder. Life can be as much fun as you let it be.

34
ATHENA & THE OLIVE TREE

The Greek goddess Athena, wise and fair, was born from the head of her father, Zeus. This came to pass because of a prophecy that any child born of Metis, goddess of wisdom, and Zeus, first among gods, would grow to be even more powerful than its father. Fearing such a fate, Zeus swallowed Metis before she could bear him a child.

Some time later, Zeus began to suffer pounding headaches, which were remedied only when his head was cleaved open by a mighty ax. Athena leapt forth, fully grown and fully armed, from her father's head. She became his favorite daughter, a patroness of the arts and a counselor of heroes.

At the time that the great city of Athens was founded, Poseidon, god of the seas, and Athena each coveted the city. To determine which god would be granted the city, the citizens decided that both Poseidon and Athena would give the new city a gift; the giver of the best gift would be awarded the city as his or her own.

Poseidon struck the earth with his triton, causing a saltwater spring to appear on the dry land. Although beautiful and impressive, the salty water was of little use to the people. Athena's gift was more subtle—an olive tree. But although the tree was small and delicate, its gifts were great: shade, olives, oil, wood. The city was given to, and named for, Athena.

The simplest gifts are often the greatest. They may be

hidden, they may seem mundane, yet these are the things that nourish our lives and give them meaning.

A SCATTERING OF LIGHT

35
THE NATURE OF OBSTACLES

The Hindu god Ganesha, the god with the elephant's head, is beloved by millions as the remover of obstacles. His name is often invoked at the beginning of a new venture; he is thought to bring his followers good luck and fortune.

He bears the head of an elephant because one day his mother, the goddess Parvati, asked him to guard the door while she bathed. He did so faithfully, denying even his father, Shiva, entrance. Shiva was not pleased at finding Ganesha standing

71

between him and Shiva's wife, and so he cut off Ganesha's head. Immediately contrite, Shiva ordered his servants to find a replacement head for Ganesha. They returned with the head of an elephant, and Ganesha has been known as the Elephant God ever since.

Elephants represent wisdom, and not just any wisdom, but the wisdom of your higher self, the self that exists before and beyond what you think of as your life. This wisdom is what counsels us to choose love, to create beauty, to forgive, to seek, to trust. This wisdom is what teaches us that all of our obstacles exist only in our minds.

Ganesha is the Remover of Obstacles, but in this well-known story, he is himself the obstacle, standing between mother and father. It is his head that is removed, and then transformed into a symbol of higher truth. This is the greatest teaching of the story: we are our obstacles. What stands between us and the love and light we seek are our thoughts, our fears and our resentments. To be free, we must replace the thoughts that stand between us and joy with the thoughts of our higher selves, our true wisdom. Only then may we be transformed into all we are capable of becoming.

Only you can remove your obstacles. Only you are the chosen hero of your story. You have the power to transform darkness into light, because darkness is nothing but the shadows of empty thoughts. Trust in your own wisdom, and allow your obstacles to be transformed.

A SCATTERING OF LIGHT

36
IMMORTALS

WE ARE TO THINK OF OURSELVES AS IMMORTALS,
DWELLING IN THE LIGHT, ENCOMPASSED AND SUSTAINED
BY SPIRITUAL POWERS. THE STEADY EFFORT TO HOLD THIS
THOUGHT WILL AWAKEN DORMANT AND UNREALIZED
POWERS, WHICH WILL UNVEIL TO US THE NEARNESS OF
THE ETERNAL.

The Yoga Sutras of Patanjali,
translated by Charles Johnston

Why do we push away the present? Why are we impatient and dissatisfied with what is before us? It is because we think our time is limited. We think that, as mere mortals, we can never have enough of all that we desire—not enough time, not enough space, not enough love. So we grab at those things we think we desire, and we push away those we think we don't want, convinced that if we do not try to control our life's experiences, our lives will be wasted.

It doesn't work. We do not find happiness by chasing it. We do not avoid pain by hiding from it. Life is too big, too complex, for the limitations we would place on it. It will not allow us to push it away.

How would you live, if you knew that you were truly an immortal? If you felt, with every fiber of your being, that you would always have all the time in the world, and more? You would stop rushing. You would stop clinging. You would allow yourself to love without fear that love would end.

And if you knew that each moment was precious and irreplaceable, even in a universe that was eternal, you would cherish it. You would embrace it. You would not try to fix, judge or hurry past it. You would live as one divine—complete in yourself, complete in the world, at peace with all that is and may be.

For just a moment, try to see the world this way. Try to see yourself as immortal, dwelling in the Light, sustained and encompassed by spiritual powers. Then try again, and again, and see what happens.

WE ARE SPIRITUAL BEINGS HAVING A HUMAN EXPERIENCE.

Pierre Teilhard de Chardin

A SCATTERING OF LIGHT

37
OF GODS & GODDESSES

What makes a god or goddess divine? If you believe the old myths and legends, the gods were not above pain, not above sorrow. They could be hurt; they could even be destroyed. So what made them divine? Simply this: knowledge of their own divinity, and the ability to transform themselves and others. Nothing is beyond the reach of a goddess, when she moves from love.

A goddess is present. Aware. Open. Sensitive to the heartbeat, the exquisite touch, texture and taste of the moment. She accepts it all, welcomes it all, knows that she cannot lose herself in any of it. She delights in the flow, the movement, the dance. She is willing to change, to grow, to expand in life, in awareness and in love. She cannot be found for she was never lost. She simply is, and therefore is all. She is in everything and everyone. To find her within is to find her without, and to know that the two are bound, connected, the same and eternal.

We all live as gods and goddesses when we claim our transformative powers. A mother, turning a child's tears to smiles with a kiss and a warm cookie. A boss, turning co-workers into a team. A hostess, turning an ordinary room into a celebration. An artist, freeing an image from clay. A woman, creating a sanctuary out of a house. Any one of us, smiling at a stranger, spreading light.

Know you are divine. Know the universe as your Beloved. Know that you can transform yourself and others. Move from love, and watch the miracles unfold.

38
WORTHY

YOU ARE A CHILD OF THE UNIVERSE, NO LESS THAN THE TREES AND THE STARS; YOU HAVE A RIGHT TO BE HERE.

Max Ehrmann

There is a reason many of us are unable to see how much we are loved, how much the universe supports us, how we are surrounded by beauty. It is because we don't think we deserve that much love, that much wonder. How could we? We are given every breath we take; we are given the freshness of a new morning, the sweetness of water, the stability of the earth beneath us. Why should all this love be ours, what could we ever do to deserve it, and what could we ever give back?

And so we think it isn't real, or isn't good enough, or we rush off into a dozen distractions without appreciating the gift of the moment. The truth is always with you. The universe needs you as much as you need it. You could not exist without sunlight, wind, water, earth; they could not exist without you. You are precious. You are irreplaceable. You are part of the mystery, the dance, the magic.

You do not need to do anything to prove yourself worthy—you already are. There is nothing you need to do or be. Notice the love around you, appreciate the gifts you are given and give thanks for the beauty without and within. Or don't—they will still be there; truth will not change. We give because it opens our hearts to more joy; we appreciate the world because it creates more joy and beauty.

This is who you are: Loved. Precious. Infinite. The more you let yourself relax into that knowledge, the more peace you will find.

Let the beauty you are be what you do.

39
OUT OF THE PAST

When we look at the world, we see our thoughts. There is nothing we see that does not have a story attached to it. The story may be a memory or it may be an opinion. Whether we are aware of it or not, we attach stories to everything we see, and those stories all arise from the past, because the past is all we know.

Our stories are not necessarily bad things. But they are only stories. To see something fresh, something new, as if for the first time, as if you had no idea what it was and no opinion about it—that is to see something truly. When you stop seeing only the past, you are open to possibility, to the future.

This is why all the sages counsel us to be here now—to stop dwelling on our thoughts of the future and the past and to be in the present. Because to be in the present, without limiting it to what you think it is or should be, is what allows you to make the best decisions, to express yourself fully, to enjoy the flow of life around you.

Enjoy your stories, but do not forget that is all they are. Let them go if they aren't serving you; create new ones. Start with where you are, and with what is possible.

Everything begins here.

MAY A FLOCK OF COLOURS, INDIGO, RED, GREEN, AND AZURE BLUE COME TO AWAKEN IN YOU A MEADOW OF DELIGHT.

John O'Donohue

ABOUT THE AUTHOR

Jennifer Wayne practiced law for seven years in Los Angeles before moving to the desert to explore another way of life. She is a graduate of the University of Arizona, Tucson, and the University of Southern California Gould School of Law.

She is currently living in La Quinta, California. For more of her writing and photography, visit her at www.scatteringlight.net.

Made in the USA
Charleston, SC
13 September 2012